Introduction

It is no secret that the "family" is in trouble in America. The foundational building block of our society is crumbling right before our eyes. And we know that Christians aren't exempt. The percentage of divorces and family breakups is basically the same among Christians as it is among non-Christians.

But there is hope. Despite the mounting pressures on families, you really can have a great marriage...you really can raise godly kids... and you can have a healthy, life-giving home life.

It will require hard work and focus but the reward is absolutely incredible. We must go back to the basics and discover God's plan for rearing a family. In this straight-shooting series, Chip Ingram will challenge the status quo and give clear and compelling help for having a great family.

The stakes are high. The future of your marriage and your kids is on the line. And it is not an overstatement to say the future of our society is on the line.

House or Home: Marriage Edition

TABLE OF CONTENTS

The fact that you are even reading this page says a lot about you. It says that you are either one of those people that has to read everything, or it says you are open to God using you to lead a group.

Leading a small group can sound intimidating, but it really doesn't have to be. Think of it more as gathering a few friends to get to know each other better and to have some discussion around spiritual matters.

Here are a few practical tips to help you get started:

1. *Pray*
One of the most important principles of spiritual leadership is to realize you can't do this on your own. No matter how long you've been a Christian or been involved in ministry, you need the power of the Holy Spirit. Lean on Him...He will help you.

2. *Invite some friends*
Don't be afraid to ask people to come to your group. You will be surprised how many people are open to a study like this. Whether you have 4 or 14 in your group, it can be a powerful experience. You should probably plan on at least an hour and a half for your group meeting.

3. *Get your materials*
You will need to get a DVD of the video teaching done by Chip Ingram. You can get the DVD from www.livingontheedge.org. Also, it will be helpful for each person to have their own study guide. You can also purchase those through the website.

4. *Be prepared to facilitate*
Just a few minutes a week in preparation can make a huge difference in the group experience. Each week preview the video teaching and review the discussion questions. If you don't think your group can get through all the questions, select the ones that are most relevant to your group.

5. *Learn to say "I don't know"*
This series takes on some of the most difficult questions that Christians and non-Christians struggle with. These sessions will spark some lively and spirited discussions. When tough questions come up, it's ok for you to say "I don't know". Take the pressure off. No one expects you to have all the answers.

6. *Love your group*
Maybe the most important thing you bring to the group is your personal care for them. If you will pray for them, encourage them, call them, e-mail them, involve them, and love them, God will be pleased and you will have a lot of fun along the way.

Thank you for your availability. May God bless you as you serve Him by serving others.

You are about to begin a powerful journey exploring God's plan for marriage and family. This powerful series taught by Chip Ingram provides in-depth teaching. This series will challenge you and provide very practical help for you and your family.

Listed below are the segments you will experience each week as well as some hints for getting the most out of this experience. If you are leading the group, you will find some additional help and leader's notes on page 71.

1. Before God

It is important for us to get "before God" and submit ourselves to his truth. During this section you will watch the video teaching by Chip. He will introduce each session with a personal word to the group followed by the teaching portion of the video. At the end of the teaching segment, Chip will wrap up the session and help the group dive into discussion.

A teaching outline with fill-ins is provided for each session. As you follow along, write down questions or insights that you can share during the discussion time.

Even though most of the verses will appear on the screen and in your notes, it is a great idea to bring your own Bible each week. It will allow you to make notes in your own Bible and find other passages that might be relevant to that week's study.

2. In Community

We not only grow by listening to God's word, but we grow "in community." The friendship and insights of those in the group will enrich your small group experience. Several discussion questions are provided for your group to further engage the teaching content. Keep the following guidelines in mind for having a healthy group discussion.

- **Be involved.** Jump in and share your thoughts. Your ideas are important and you have a perspective that is unique and can benefit the other group members.

- **Be a good listener.** Value what others are sharing. Seek to really understand the perspective of others in your group and don't be afraid to ask follow up questions.

- **Be courteous.** People hold strong opinions about the topics in this study. Spirited discussion is great. Disrespect and attack is not. When there is disagreement, focus on the issue and never turn the discussion into a personal attack.

- **Be focused.** Stay on topic. Help the group explore the subject at hand and try to save unrelated questions or stories for afterwards.

- **Be careful not to dominate.** Be aware of the amount of talking you are doing in proportion to the rest of the group and make space for others to speak.

- **Be a learner.** Stay sensitive to what God might be wanting to teach you through the lesson, as well as through what others have to say. Focus more on your own growth rather than making a point or winning an argument.

3. On Mission

One reason we get "before God" and live "in community" is so that we can be "on mission." Our faith has an external component. We are called to be salt and light by living out our faith in the real world. This section provides some simple suggestions to help the lesson come to life. Don't ignore them; give them a try!

4. Action Step

Sometimes at the end of the session you will find an "Action Step." The action steps are not so much about reaching out to others as they are about putting into practice what you are learning. These action steps help you to become "doers" of the word, not just "hearers" of the word.

marriage: a holy
covenant

Part 1

A Harris Poll among college students asked "what's the key to happiness?" _____ said the key to long term happiness is a "close knit family."

THE CURRENT CONDITION OF THE AMERICAN FAMILY

- Only 25% of families in America have a mom and dad in the home with the kids.

- 1/3 of all the people who go through divorce will live below the poverty level.

- 60% of all people live together before they get married.

- Over half of all the children born this year will be born out of wedlock.

- Coming from a broken home, especially one in which the father is absent, is the highest predictability factor for:

   Poverty

   Violence

   Future felonies

   Depression

   Teen suicide

   Promiscuity

   Gang involvement

   Drug use

- Experts attribute the primary cause of family disintegration to the increased failure to hold marriage and marriage commitments in high esteem.

- _____ of all sexual acts on television are between two people who are not married.

GOD'S BLUEPRINT FOR MARRIAGE

*For this reason a man will leave his father and mother
and be united to his wife and they will become one flesh.*

GENESIS 2:24 (NIV)

The man and his wife were both naked and felt no shame.

GENESIS 2:25 (NIV)

They were not only naked physically, but also _____

and _____.

Marriage — A Holy _____

GOD

MAN ←——————————————————→ WOMAN

1. Marriage is _____ idea.

2. The goal of marriage is _____.

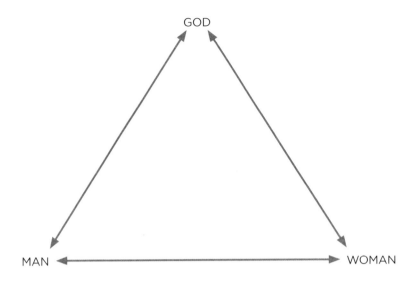

GOD

MAN ⟷ WOMAN

3 Aspects of Oneness

1. Spiritual — _____

2. Soul — _____

3. Physical — _____

In Community ———————————————

1. When you were growing up, what characterized the marriages you observed?

2. If you are married, share how you met, how long you have been married and what first attracted you to your spouse.

3. From all the information and facts Chip shared, what was most alarming or surprising to you?

4. As you think about the current condition of the "family" in America, what are you most concerned about? Why?

5. Since getting married, what has been the single biggest change in your own understanding of marriage?

6. Have someone in the group read Genesis 2:18-25. What are some foundational truths in this passage that help us understand God's view of marriage?

7. Chip talked about 3 aspects of "oneness" in our marriage — spiritual, soul, and physical. What could you do to have better spiritual "oneness" (intimacy) with your spouse?

marriage: a holy covenant

Part 2

Observations about Marriage

1. Marriage is God's idea (covered in session 1).

2. The goal of marriage is oneness (covered in session 1).

3. The _____ of marriage.

The closer you get to God the closer you will get to your spouse.

MARRIAGE IS A HOLY _____

> *For what reason? Because the Lord has been witness between you and the wife of your youth, against whom you have dealt treacherously thought she is your companion and your wife by covenant.*
>
> MALACHI 2:14 (NIV)

Marriage is not a _____ between two people;
it is a covenant.

> *When you make a vow to God, do not delay in fulfilling it. He has no pleasure in fools; fulfill your vow. It is better not to make a vow than to make one and not fulfill it.*
>
> ECCLESIASTES 5:4-5 (NIV)

A covenant is an agreement and a _____ one person makes with another.

4 ASPECTS OF A COVENANT

1. It is initiated by a _____ .

2. The _____ are outlined.

3. It is ratified by _____ .

4. There is a _____ .

Vows are serious and _____ is awesome.

IMPLICATIONS OF THE COVENANT

1. _____ is not an option (Malachi 2).

2. _____ is a serious, covenant breaking offense (Proverbs 2:16-19).

3. Sex _____ is a violation of this holy covenant.

4. _____ relationships are forbidden as a violation of God's design.

1. Who do you know that has really modeled a "covenant" marriage? In your opinion, what qualities do you observe in their relationship that makes you say their marriage is strong?

2. Read Malachi 2:13-16. What most stands out to you in this passage? Why?

3. Twice in the passage in Malachi, the prophet says "so guard yourself in your spirit and do not break faith." For you personally, what does it look like for you to guard your spirit when it comes to your marriage?

4. As you heard Chip speak passionately about the seriousness and permanency of the marriage covenant, what was your response?

5. Chip made the statement "vows are serious and mercy is awesome." Spend some time unpacking that statement. What does it mean and what are the implications of that statement?

6. Chip said that adultery is a serious, covenant breaking offense. Read Proverbs 6:20-29. What verse or truth most stands out to you in this passage? Why?

7. Close your group meeting this week by spending some time praying for the marriages in your group.

On Mission

Take action this week on Chip's statement that "vows are serious and mercy is awesome." Extend God's grace and mercy to someone going through a difficult marriage situation. Shoot them an e-mail, send them a card or take them out to lunch just to let them know you care.

is there a man in
the house?

Part 1

THE EVOLUTION OF THE AMERICAN MALE

1950's — A "father-absent" family was unheard of

1960's — Sexual revolution — separated sex from responsibility

1970's — Feminist movement — redefined the roles of women and men

1980's — Success, money and materialism

1990's — Confusion as the family began to break down

U.S. Commission on Child Development (late 1990's)...

> Never before in one generation of America have teenagers been less healthy, less cared for, or less prepared for life.. This occurrence, mind you, occurred in the most affluent, privileged nation in the history of the world. It is a direct result of marital disintegration and the related forces working against the family.

> Young men without fathers are twice as likely to drop out of school and go to jail. They are four times as likely to need treatment for emotional behavior problems.

2 PC's WE MUST AVOID

1. Politically _____ — lack of manliness and
    confused roles.

2. _____ -Christian — dominant and abusive.

REDEFINING MANHOOD IN OUR MARRIAGES AND HOMES

- It begins with _____ submission.

Be subject to one another in the fear of Christ.

EPHESIANS 5:21 (NASB)

Submission = historically had the idea of being under the command of a commanding officer.

- The _____ of marriage is God.

- Mutual submission is the _____ itself.

GREAT MARRIAGES REQUIRE CLARITY OF ROLES

Wives, be subject to your own husbands, as to the Lord. For the husband is the head of the wife, as Christ also is the head of the church, He Himself being the Savior of the body. But as the church is subject to Christ, so also the wives ought to be to their husbands in everything.

Husbands, love your wives, just as Christ also loved the church and gave Himself up for her, so that He might sanctify her, having cleansed her by the washing of water with the Word, that He might present to Himself the church in all her glory, having no spot or wrinkle or any such thing; but that she would be holy and blameless. So husbands ought also to love their own wives as their own bodies. He who loves his own wife loves himself, for no one ever hated his own flesh, but nourishes and cherishes it, just as Christ also does the church, because we are members of His body.

EPHESIANS 5:22-30 (NASB)

2 WAYS TO LOVE YOUR WIFE AS CHRIST LOVED THE CHURCH

1. You _____ her.

2. You _____ her.

In Community

1. Describe your relationship with your dad growing up? How would you describe your dad's role in your home? If you didn't grow up with a dad, describe the most significant male influence in your life.

2. How have you personally seen the role of men change in your lifetime?

3. In Ephesians 5, Paul used the analogy of Christ's love for the church to illustrate how a man is to love his wife. As a group, brainstorm a list of ways that Christ shows his love for the church. Get specific and think of passages that demonstrate Christ's love for the church.

4.   Chip talked about "mutual submission" in marriage. What is one way that you need to submit to your spouse?

5.   Chip said that husbands are to "nourish" their wives and help them grow and develop. Ladies, what is one area where your husband could help support you and encourage your growth?

6.   Husbands are also to cherish their wives. Men, what is one way that you could better "cherish" your wife?

7.   As Chip said, husbands have an impossible job and can't possibly love their wives as Christ loved the church without God's help. So, close this session by praying for the men in your group. Wives, pray over and for your husbands.

Action Step

Men, take the initiative this week to practically demonstrate how much you cherish your wife. Get creative!

is there a man in the house?

Part 2

Husbands are to step up.

DIAGNOSTIC QUESTIONS

1. Who initiates spiritual growth in your home?

2. Who handles the money in your home?

3. Who disciplines the children when you're both at home?

4. Who initiates talking about problems, future plans, and areas of development?

5. Who asks the most questions in your home and who gives the most statements?

6. When you are together, who drives the car?

THREE WAYS TO STEP UP

1. Husbands must love their wives _____ .

   • Love your wife at the cost of your _____ .

   • Love your wife at the cost of your _____ .

2. Husbands must love their wives with _____ .

   Purposefully seek to develop your wife's greatest strength, beauty and gifts.

3.　Husbands must love their wives _____ .

*For additional help with your marriage, you want to check out the curriculum, **Experiencing God's Dream for Your Marriage** (livingontheedge.org/store)*

WHAT LOVING YOUR WIFE DOESN'T MEAN

1.　You _____ what your wife wants.

Love means you do what's best for the other person.

2.　You don't have a _____ of your own.

3.　You make her _____ on you.

4.　You call all the _____ .

1. What is one way you have seen your husband step up in your marriage and in your home?

2. At the beginning of this session, Chip asked six diagnostic questions. Choose one of the six questions and answer it from the perspective of what you saw in your parent's roles growing up.

3. Husbands, from those six diagnostic questions, which one do you need to work on? Share one practical way you could begin to take greater leadership in that area.

4. Chip talked about having a plan to strengthen your marriage. If you and your spouse were to sit down and put together a plan to strengthen your marriage, what is one thing you would like to see in the plan?

5. Husbands must love their wives sensitively. Ladies, what is it, that when your husband does it, really makes you feel loved?

6. Chip said that husbands need a life outside their marriage. Men, what do you enjoy doing that is life-giving to you? How well are you doing at balancing outside interests and focusing on your marriage?

7. Chip closed this session by saying that true spiritual leadership doesn't mean that the husband calls all the shots. Share a little about how you and your spouse make decisions when the two of you can't agree.

Action Step

This week set aside some time for an honest and helpful discussion with your spouse. Discuss the six diagnostic questions from this session and any possible adjustments you might need to make in your home.

is there a woman in the home?

Part 1

THE DIFFERENCE BETWEEN FEMINISM AND RADICAL FEMINISM

Feminism — The principle that women should have political, economic, and social rights equal to men. (Webster's Dictionary)

Radical Feminism — "Now is the time to drop a boot heel in the groin of patriarchy. Now is the time to fight back! Now listen to who the enemies are: no god, no master, and no laws!" (National Organization of Women)

THE CHANGING ROLES OF WOMEN

- In 1920's less than 20% of women (age 20-50) worked outside the home.

- By 1960 40% of women worked outside the home.

- By 1970 50% of women worked outside the home.

- By 1990 75% of women worked outside the home.

REDEFINING WOMANHOOD

- It begins with _____ submission.

- Submission addresses _____ not value, equality or importance.

The supreme example is the submission of Jesus to His heavenly Father.

Now I want you to realize that the head of every man is Christ, and the head of the woman is man, and the head of Christ is God.

1 CORINTHIANS 11:3 (NIV)

A GREAT DANCE REQUIRES CLARITY

> *Wives, be subject to your own husbands, as to the Lord. For the husband is the head of the wife as Christ also is head of the church, He Himself being the Savior of the body. But as the church is subject to Christ, so also wives ought to be to their husbands in everything.*
>
> EPHESIANS 5:22-24 (NASB)

Men need to "step up" and Women need to "_____."

Man's greatest fear is _____.

Woman's greatest fear is relational _____.

> *Husbands, love your wives, just as Christ also loved the church and gave Himself up for her, so that He might sanctify her, having cleansed her by the washing of water with the word, that He might present to Himself the church in all her glory, having no spot or wrinkle or any such thing; but that she would be holy and blameless.*
>
> EPHESIANS 5:25-27 (NASB)

So husbands ought also to love their own wives as their own bodies. He who loves his own wife loves himself; for no one ever hated his own flesh, but nourishes and cherishes it, just as Christ also does the church, because we are members of His body. For this reason a man shall leave his father and mother and shall be joined to his wife, and the two shall become one flesh.

EPHESIANS 5:28-31 (NASB)

In Community

1. How is your role as a woman today (or for the guys, how is your wife's role) different than your mom's was a generation ago?

2. Describe your relationship with your mom growing up. How did it shape you?

3. How would you describe your mom's role in your home? If you didn't grow up with a dad, describe the most significant male influence in your life.

4. What is one way you are doing the "marriage dance" better today than when you first got married?

5. Chip said women need to "step in without stepping over their husbands." What would that look like practically?

6. Chip said that a woman's greatest struggle is control. Do you agree or disagree? Why or why not?

7. Ladies, what is one way that you could better submit to your husband?

8. Close this session by praying for the women in your group. Husbands, pray over and for your wives.

Action Step ───────────────────────────

One of the most powerful things you can do as a couple is pray together. Commit to praying together at least 3 days this week.

is there a woman in
the home?

Part 2

THE VIEW OF WOMEN IN ANCIENT TIMES

- Jews looked on a wife as a servant. In their prayers, Jewish men thanked God they were not women.

- Greeks viewed women as objects for their sexual pleasure and to manage a man's household. Prostitution was rampant.

- Romans viewed women as disposable and dispensable. Divorce was the rule, not the exception.

- Therefore, the teaching of Ephesians 5 elevates and emancipates women.

WHAT SUBMISSION LOOKS LIKE

1. Wives are to step in and support, affirm, and encourage their husbands with strength and respect to lead their families in righteousness.

2. Wives must _____ support their husbands from the heart as an act of obedience to Christ.

3. Submission has less to do with you and your husband and more to do with you and _____ .

4. Wives must believe that submission is a woman's greatest ally and the key to bringing _____ .

Wives, in the same way be submissive to your husbands so that, if any of them do not believe the word, they may be won over without words by the behavior of their wives, when they see the purity and reverence of your lives. Your beauty should not come from outward adornment, such as braided hair and the wearing of gold jewelry and fine clothes. Instead, it should be that of your inner self, the unfading beauty of a gentle and quiet spirit, which is of great worth in God's sight. For this is the way the holy women of the past who put their hope in God used to make themselves beautiful. They were submissive to their own husbands.

1 PETER 3:1-5 (NIV)

SUBMISSION DOES NOT MEAN THAT YOU...

1. Are to be passive or feel _____.

2. Submit _____ when you think he's right.

3. _____ Scripture, reason, or morality to support your husband.

4. Are a _____.

5. Use submission as a _____ to get your way.

1. Men, share two specific things that you deeply appreciate about your wife.

2. Wives, what is one practical way you could support, affirm, or encourage your husband?

3. Read 1 Peter 3:1-5. In verse 2 Peter talks about wives living pure and reverent lives? How would you define a "pure and reverent" life?

4. In this passage Peter talks about the beauty of the "inner self." Why do you think so many women struggle with this issue?

5. Wives, how big of a struggle is this for you and what can your husband do to help with this struggle?

6. 1 Peter 3:5 says "For this is the way the holy women of the past who put their hope in God used to adorn themselves." What does putting your hope in God have to do with submission?

7. Read Proverbs 31:10-31. What quality from the "noble wife" do you most admire?

Action Step

For the women: This week reflect and meditate on Proverbs 31:10-31.

For the men: Pray every day this week for your wife.

what's a man
to do?

Part 1

A Man's Top 3 Priorities (Ephesians 5:22-31)

- Provide

- Protect

- Nurture

3 KEY PASSAGES FOR MEN

> *If anyone does not provide for his own, and especially for those of his household, he has denied the faith and is worse than an unbeliever.*
>
> 1 TIMOTHY 5:8 (NASB)

> *You husbands in the same way, live with your wives in an understanding way, as with someone weaker, since she is a woman; and show her honor as a fellow heir of the grace of life, so that your prayers will not be hindered.*
>
> 1 PETER 3:7 (NASB)

> *but if a man does not know how to manage his own household, how will he take care of the church of God?*
>
> 1 TIMOTHY 3:5 (NASB)

HOW DOES A MAN STEP UP AND LEAD HIS FAMILY?

3 Primary Responsibilities

1.   a.   Financial Provision for the Family

- Do _____ work.

- Honor God _____ .

- Live within your _____ .

- Prepare for the _____ .

    10% — God

    80% — Living expenses

    10% — Savings

- _____ your children.

    b.   Core Financial Values to Model and Teach

- Work ethic
- Stewardship of money and time
- Responsibility and disciplines
- Enjoyment and generosity

2.   _____ Development and Protection of the Family

Husbands, in the same way be considerate as you live with your wives, and treat them with respect as the weaker partner and as heirs with you of the gracious gift of life, so that nothing will hinder your prayers.

1 PETER 3:7 (NIV)

Fathers, do not exasperate your children; instead, bring them up in the training and instruction of the Lord.

EPHESIANS 6:4 (NIV)

Hear, O Israel: The LORD our God, the LORD is one. Love the LORD your God with all your heart and with all your soul and with all your strength. These commandments that I give you today are to be on your hearts. Impress them on your children. Talk about them when you sit at home and when you walk along the road, when you lie down and when you get up. Tie them as symbols on your hands and bind them on your foreheads. Write them on the doorframes of your houses and on your gates.

DEUTERONOMY 6:4-9 (NIV)

3. As men, we are the family priest.

Practical Objectives of Being The Priest of Your Home

- Set the pace _____ .

- Know the _____ of your wife and children.

- _____ for them and with them regularly.

1. What does it look like for you to be the spiritual leader in your home? Wives, how can you help your husbands in this role?

2. 1 Peter 3:7 says you are to show your wife "honor as a fellow heir of the grace of life." Husbands, share one very specific way that you can show your wife "honor."

3. Chip said that part of a man's responsibility is to help the family prepare for the future. Is there something you and your spouse need to do in order to better be prepared for the future?

4. If you still have kids at home, which of the 4 Core Financial Values do you need to focus on with your kids? If your kids are grown, what piece of advice would you pass on to other parents?

5. Read Deuteronomy 6:4-9. As a group, brainstorm a list of principles from this passage that would help us spiritually develop our kids.

6. What is one specific way you could apply Deuteronomy 6:4-9 in your family?

7. For us to effectively develop our children spiritually, Chip said we must set the pace personally. For husbands and wives, honestly share how you are doing at maintaining your personal walk with God.

   What would help you take your personal relationship with God to the next level?

Action Step

As a couple sit down this week and have a discussion about the spiritual development of your children. Come up with a couple of clear action steps that you can implement. By the way, even if your kids are grown, you can still be intentional to invest in their development.

what's a man to do?

Part 2

- Ensure that biblical instruction occurs at home as well as at church.

- Make experiencing God and loving each other your aim.

SPIRITUAL CORE VALUES TO DEVELOP

- _____ evidenced by prayer and occasional fasting.

- Faith in God's _____ .

- _____ outreach and orientation.

- Progressive growth in personal _____ .

3. Relational Health and Welfare of the Family

The responsibility is to manage the household in a manner that produces love, obedience, and respect toward God and one another.

- Verbalize and _____ the marriage covenant.

- _____ to develop marriage and family relationships.

- Provide structure and _____ to ensure that family relationships take priority over outside demands.

- Make sure that _____ is built into the fabric and rhythm of the family schedule.

- Exercise _____ fairly, firmly, and lovingly among all family members.

Relational Core Values

- Model and teach unconditional acceptance.

- Give affirmation that's specific and consistent.

- Offer accountability that's filled with truth and grace.

- Teach your kids to resolve conflict, to speak the truth in love.

In Community

1. How are you doing with this one? What can you do to be more proactive in making your family and marriage a top priority?

2. Chip challenged us to "ensure that biblical instruction occurs at home." In light of your current season of life, what would be some practical strategies for doing this?

3. One of the core values we are to develop in our families is that of "serving." Brainstorm with your group some practical ways that your family could serve your local community.

4. Chip talked about the responsibility we have for "personal holiness" in our families. Where do you need to be careful that your family doesn't conform to the ways of the world?

5. What do you need to do in order to more proactively promote personal holiness in your family?

6. Many families are stressed and exhausted because they are overcommitted. Is there something you need to cut out so that family relationships can take a higher priority? What step do you need to take?

7. At the end of this session, Chip talked about 4 Relational Core Values. Which of these 4 have you done a good job with? Which one could you work on and what is a practical way you could do that?

On Mission

As a family, do a project where your entire family could help serve somebody else in need in your community.

what's a woman to do?

Part 1

THE RESPONSIBILITY OF A WOMAN

The What? Step in and _____ .

The How? A Woman's Top 3 Priorities

- _____

    Create a relational environment that promotes the spiritual, emotional, and physical welfare of those around her.

- _____

    Minimize the harmful influences and effects upon the lives she has been entrusted to nurture.

- _____

    Maximize all available spiritual, emotional, and physical resources and relationships to do good to the people that you are assigned to care for.

Three Key Passages

An excellent wife, who can find? For her worth is far above jewels. The heart of her husband trusts in her, and he will have no lack of gain. She does him good and not evil all the days of her life.

PROVERBS 31:10-12 (NASB)

I would prefer that young widows get married, have children, and look after their families. Then the enemy won't have any reason to say insulting things about us.

1 TIMOTHY 5:14 (CEV)

Older women likewise are to be reverent in their behavior, not malicious gossips nor enslaved to much wine, teaching what is good, so that they may encourage the young women to love their husbands, to love their children, to be sensible, pure, workers at home, kind, being subject to their own husbands, so that the word of God will not be dishonored.

TITUS 2:3-5 (NASB)

The Christian home is to be a picture of the love of Christ _____ .

A WOMAN'S RESPONSIBILITY TO HER MARRIAGE

1. A wife's #1 priority is to support, affirm, and empower her husband to fulfill his God given calling both within and outside the church.

What Does This Look Like Practically?

- _____ to be with God.

- _____ for your husband.

2. A woman's influence is often as informal as it is formal, indirect as it is direct.

- _____ for your husband daily.

- _____ for your husband daily.

- _____ your time with your husband.

For the first part of the discussion this week, split up into two groups; one for men and one for women.

WOMEN

1. Is your husband the #1 priority in your life?

2. What specific things can you do to affirm and encourage him?

3. What is your biggest challenge in trying to be the woman God wants you to be for your family?

4. What is the most significant adjustment you sense that God might be asking you to make?

5. Before getting back together with the whole group, spend time praying for the other women in your group.

6. Titus challenged the older women to invest in the younger women and teach them to love their husbands and their children. Ladies, if you could sit down with a younger married woman, what one piece of advice would you give them for having a great marriage or being a great mom?

MEN

1. What does your wife currently do to affirm and encourage you?

2. What are the top 5 things your wife could do to help you feel important and loved?

3. What is your biggest challenge in trying to be the man God wants you to be for your family?

4. What is the most significant adjustment you sense that God might be asking you to make?

5. Before getting back together with the whole group, spend time praying for the other men in your group. Then, get back together with the whole group for the last part of the discussion.

6. Men, if you could sit down with a younger man, what one piece of advice would you give them for having a great marriage or being a great dad?

On Mission

This week consider blessing a younger married couple that you know. Maybe it is buying their dinner or taking care of their kids while they have a date night. Maybe it is having them over to your home for dinner and just getting to know them. Get creative!

what's a woman to do?

Part 2

A Woman's Responsibility to Her Children

(Continued from part 1)

2. Create an environment in the home that nurtures and develops her children to fulfill God's will for their lives.

What does this look like practically?

- Model _____ on Christ.

    2 Great Temptations for Moms:
    - Overcompensate
    - Overprotect

- Pray for your children _____ .

- Create _____ and schedules that make family life a priority.

- Speed kills relationships.

- Teach your children how to _____ .

    Skills to teach our kids:

    Read

    Pray

    Cook

    Listen

Celebrate

Be generous

Do a craft

Talk (communicate)

Resolve conflict

To write

Play an instrument

Play a sport

Relax

- Be _____ .

3. Train younger women in the art of becoming a Godly wife and mother.

In Community

1. From this entire series, what is the biggest takeaway for you? Is there a radical or drastic step that you sense God might be asking you to take?

2. As you think back to your childhood, how did your mom nurture and develop you?

3. Husbands, in what ways have you seen your wife nurture and develop your children?

4. Chip said "That which is hoped for but not scheduled, rarely happens." What is something you hope for in your family that needs to get scheduled and on your calendar?

5. What are some meaningful traditions that you have or want to have for your family?

6. Chip gave a list of ways to teach your children how to live. From his list or your own list, what are 2 or 3 things you want to be sure and teach your kids?

7. Close this week's session by praying for the children of the families in your group.

People come to groups with a variety of different expectations. The purpose of a group agreement is simply to make sure everyone is on the same page and that we have some common expectations.

The following Group Agreement is a tool to help you discuss specific guidelines during your first meeting. Modify anything that does not work for your group, then be sure to discuss the questions in the section called Our Game Plan. This will help you to have an even greater group experience!

WE AGREE TO THE FOLLOWING PRIORITIES

- **Take the Bible Seriously** — Seek to understand and apply God's truth in the Bible.

- **Group Attendance** — Give priority to the group meeting (Call if I am going to be absent or late).

- **Safe Environment** — Create a safe place where people can be heard and feel loved (no snap judgments or simple fixes).

- **Respectful Discussion** — Speak in a respectful and honoring way to our mate and others in the group.

- **Be Confidential** — Keep anything that is shared strictly confidential and within the group.

- **Spiritual Health** — Give group members permission to help me live a godly, healthy spiritual life that is pleasing to God.

- **Building Relationships** — Get to know the other members of the group and pray for them regularly.

- **Prayer** — Regularly pray with and for each other.

- **Other**

OUR GAME PLAN

1. What will we do for refreshments?

2. What will we do about childcare?

3. What day and time will we meet?

4. Where will we meet?

5. How long will we meet each week?

BEFORE THE GROUP ARRIVES

1. **Be prepared.** Your personal preparation can make a huge difference in the quality of the group experience. We strongly suggest previewing both the DVD teaching by Chip Ingram and the study guide.

2. **Pray for your group members by name.** Ask God to use your time together to touch the heart of every person in your group. Expect God to challenge and change people as a result of this study.

3. **Provide refreshments.** There's nothing like food to help a group relax and connect with each other. For the first week, we suggest you prepare a snack, but after that, ask other group members to bring the food so that they share in the responsibilities of the group and make a commitment to return.

4. **Relax.** Don't try to imitate someone else's style of leading a group. Lead the group in a way that fits your style and temperament. Remember that people may feel nervous showing up for a small group study, so put them at ease when they arrive. Make sure to have all the details covered prior to your group meeting, so that once people start arriving, you can focus on them.

Before God (WATCH THE VIDEO)

1. **Get the video ready.** Each video session on the DVD will have 3 components. The first couple of minutes Chip will introduce this week's topic Then, you will watch the actual teaching content that Chip taught in front of a live audience. This portion of the video will be roughly 20-30 minutes in length. Finally, Chip will then share some closing thoughts and set up the discussion time for your group.

2. **Test the equipment.** Be sure to test your video equipment ahead of time and make sure you have located this week's lesson on the DVD menu. The video segments flow from one right into the next. So, once you start the session, you won't have to stop the video until Chip has finished his closing thoughts and prepared the group for the first discussion question.

3. **Have ample materials.** Before you start the video, also make sure everyone has their own copy of the study guide. Encourage the group to open to this week's session and follow along with the teaching. There is an outline in the study guide with an opportunity to fill in the outline.

4. **Arrange the room.** Set up the chairs in the room so that everyone can see the television. And, arrange the room in such a way that it is conducive to discussion.

In Community

Here are some guidelines for leading the discussion time:

1. **Make this a discussion, not a lecture.** Resist the temptation to do all the talking, and to answer your own questions. Don't be afraid of a few moments of silence while people formulate their answers.

   Don't feel like you need to have all the answers. There is nothing wrong with simply saying "I don't know the answer to that, but I'll see if I can find an answer this week."

2. **Encourage everyone to participate.** Don't let one person dominate, but also don't pressure quieter members to speak during the first couple of sessions. Be patient. Ask good follow up questions and be sensitive to delicate issues.

3. **Affirm people's participation and input.** If an answer is clearly wrong, ask "What led you to that conclusion?" or ask what the rest of the group thinks. If a disagreement arises, don't be too quick to shut it down! The discussion can draw out important perspectives, and if you can't resolve it there, offer to research it further and return to the issue next week.

   However, if someone goes on the offensive and engages in personal attack, you will need to step in as the leader. In the midst of spirited discussion, we must also remember that people are fragile and there is no place for disrespect.

4. **Detour when necessary.** If an important question is raised that is not in the study guide, take time to discuss it. Also, if someone shares something personal and emotional, take time for them. Stop and pray for them right then. Allow the Holy Spirit room to maneuver, and follow his prompting when the discussion changes direction.

5. **Subgroup.** One of the principles of small group life is "when numbers go up, sharing goes down." So, if you have a large group, sometimes you may want to split up into groups of 4-6 for the discussion time. This is a great way to give everyone, even the quieter members, a chance to share. Choose someone in the group to guide each of the smaller groups through the discussion. This involves others in the leadership of the group, and provides an opportunity for training new leaders.

6. **Prayer.** One of the principles of small group life is "when numbers go up, sharing goes down." So, if you have a large group, sometimes you may want to split up into groups of 4-6 for the discussion time. This is a great way to give everyone, even the quieter members, a chance to share. Choose someone in the group to guide each of the smaller groups through the discussion. This involves others in the leadership of the group, and provides an opportunity for training new leaders.

On Mission

These simple suggestions will help the group apply the lesson. Be sure and leave adequate time to talk about these practical applications of the lesson. Most of these assignments involve an action step that will encourage the group to put into practice what they are learning. Occasionally ask people if they have been working on these assignments and what the results have been.

Action Step

Some of these assignments involve an action step that will encourage the group to put into practice what they are learning. Occasionally ask people if they have been working on these assignments and what the results have been.

LEADER'S NOTES

Thanks for hosting this series called *House or Home*. This practical series will help you discover God's plan for a great marriage and family. Whether you are brand new at leading a small group or you are a seasoned veteran, God is going to use you. God has a long history of using ordinary people to get His work done.

These brief notes are intended to help prepare you for each week's session. By spending just a few minutes each week previewing the video and going over these leader notes you will set the table for a great group experience. Also, don't forget to pray for your group each week.

SESSION 1: marriage: a holy covenant (part 1)

- If your group doesn't know each other well, be sure that you spend some time getting acquainted. Don't rush right into the video lesson. Remember, small groups are not just about a study or a meeting, they are about relationships.

- Be sure to capture everyone's contact information. It is a good idea to send out an e-mail with everybody's contact information so that the group can stay in touch. At the back of your study guide is a roster where people can fill in the names and contact information of the other group members.

- When you are ready to start the session, be sure that each person in your group has a copy of the study guide. The small group study guide is important for people to follow along and to take notes.

- The video lesson taught by Chip Ingram will be about 20-30 minutes in length. So, you will have plenty of time for discussion. Each session opens with Chip setting up the lesson. Then, the video will transition to his live teaching. And, at the end of the teaching Chip will come back and wrap up the session as well as set up the first discussion question for the group.

- Facilitating the discussion time. Several times Chip will ask you as the facilitator to lead the way by answering the first question. This allows you to lead by example and your willingness to share openly about your life will help others feel the permission to do the same.

- In this first session Chip will talk about God's design for marriage and the sacred commitment between a man and a woman. Be sensitive to the fact that some couples might really be struggling in their marriage. Let people know it's ok to share whatever they are comfortable sharing. Make sure no one feels coerced or cornered into sharing more than they are ready to.

SESSION 2: marriage: a holy covenant (part 2)

- Why not begin your preparation by praying right now for the people in your group. You might even want to keep their names in your Bible. You may also want to ask people in your group how you can pray for them specifically.

- If somebody doesn't come back this week, be sure and follow up with them. Even if you knew they were going to have to miss the group meeting, give them a call or send them an e-mail letting them know that they were missed. It would also be appropriate to have a couple of other people in the group let them know they were missed.

- If you haven't already previewed the video, take the time to do so. It will help you know how to best facilitate the group and what the best discussion questions are for your group.

- Be sure this week to preview the last couple of minutes of this week's video teaching. Chip delivers a serious, intense plea to build a covenant marriage. Save a little time at the end of this week's meeting for prayer. You could do this prayer time as an entire group or you might consider having couples pray together.

- During this week's session you will find an "On Mission" assignment. Take the last few minutes of your meeting to review this suggested application of this week's lesson. Encourage your group to reach out to someone who is going through a difficult marriage situation.

SESSION 3: is there a man in the house? (part 1)

- Did anybody miss last week's session? If so, make it a priority to follow up and let them know they were missed. It just might be your care for them that keeps them connected to the group.

- Share the load. One of the ways to raise the sense of ownership within the group is to get them involved in more than coming to the meeting. So, get someone to help with refreshments... find somebody else to be in charge of the prayer requests... get someone else to be in charge of any social gathering you plan... let someone else lead the discussion one night. Give away as much of the responsibility as possible. That is GOOD leadership.

- Think about last week's meeting for a moment. Was there anyone that didn't talk or participate? In every group there are extroverts and there are introverts. There are people who like to talk and then there are those who are quite content NOT to talk. Not everyone engages in the same way or at the same level, but you do want to try and create an environment where everyone wants to participate.

- Follow up with your group this week to see how they did with the "On Mission" assignment of reaching out to another couple that might be struggling in their marriage.

- You will notice that the last discussion question encourages a time of prayer for the men in your group. You could have a group prayer time praying for the men in your group, but it would be very meaningful to have wives individually pray over their husbands. As the leader, you will need to determine whether this is within the comfort level of your group.

SESSION 4: is there a man in the house? (part 2)

- Don't feel any pressure to get through all the questions. As people open up and talk, don't move on too quickly. Give them the space to what is going on inside them as they interact with this teaching.

- Don't be afraid of silence. When you ask people a question, give them time to think about it. Don't feel like you have to fill every quiet moment with words.

- If your group is not sharing as much as you would like or if the discussion is being dominated by a person or two, try subgrouping. If your group is 8 people or more, this is a great way to up the level of participation.

- After watching the video teaching, divide the group into a couple of smaller groups for the discussion time. It is good to get someone you think would be a good facilitator to agree to this ahead of time.

- During this session, Chip continues his teaching about the role of men. Many men feel inadequate as the spiritual leader of their home. So, as much as possible, make sure every wife answers question number one. Their husbands will be encouraged.

- Really encourage the couples this week to implement the "Action Step" at the end of the discussion questions. Challenge them to set aside at least an hour for this important conversation.

SESSION 5: is there a woman in the home? (part 1)

- Confidentiality is crucial to group life. The moment trust is breached, people will shut down and close up. So, you may want to mention the importance of confidentiality again this week just to keep it on people's radar.

- Each time your group meets take a few minutes to update on what has happened since the last group meeting. Ask people what they are learning and putting into practice. Remember, being a disciple of Jesus means becoming a "doer of the Word."

- The last question this week has you read from Proverbs 31:10-31. It might be good to look over a couple of translations and then be prepared to read the passage out loud to the group.

- In session 3 you had the wives pray over their husbands. In this session, close by having the men pray over their wives. This can be a very tender and special time for the couples in your group.

- Most couples do not pray together. So, the recommended "Action Step" this week could provide a spiritual breakthrough. Be sure to challenge your group to take on the challenge of praying together as a couple three times this week.

SESSION 6: is there a woman in the home? (part 2)

- You are now at the halfway point of this series. How is it going? How well is the group connecting? What has been going well and what needs a little work? Are there any adjustments you need to make?

- One way to deepen the level of community within your group is to spend time together outside the group meeting. If you have not already done so, plan something that will allow you to get to know each other better. Also, consider having someone else in the group take responsibility for your fellowship event.

- As you begin this week's session, do a check-in to see what people are learning and applying from this series. Don't be afraid to take some time at the beginning of your meeting to review some key ideas from the previous week's lessons.

- This week Chip will continue to shine the spotlight on the role of a woman in the home. He will talk further about a wife's submission to her husband. As you know, this can be a delicate and sensitive topic. One way to set the right tone for the discussion is to have all the men answer the question about what they deeply appreciate about their wife.

- Question number five this week could be very difficult for some of the wives in your group. Depending on their level of honesty, this question could also surface some of the broken places in their marriage that keeps them from wanting to be submissive.

SESSION 7: what's a man to do? (part 1)

- Consider asking someone in your group to facilitate next week's lesson. Who knows, there might be a great potential small group leader in your group. It will give you a break and give them a chance to grow.

- Consider sending an e-mail to each person in your group this week letting them know you prayed for them today. Also, let them know that you are grateful that they are in the group.

- Take a few minutes this week before you get into the study to talk about the impact of this series so far. Ask people what they are learning, applying, and changing in their lives. For this series to have lasting impact it has to be more than just absorbing information. So, challenge your group to put what they are learning into action.

- This week's lesson is largely about a man's spiritual leadership in his home. Be sure and leave time for questions five and six. These questions ask the group to dig into Deuteronomy 6:4-9 to find help in knowing how to spiritually develop our kids. You might want to have two or three Bibles available for people to use for this part of the discussion.

SESSION 8: what's a man to do? (part 2)

- Follow up questions. The only thing better than good questions are good follow up questions. Questions are like onions. Each question allows another layer to be peeled back and get beneath the surface.

- In your group meetings be sure to take adequate time for prayer. Don't just tack it on at the end of the meeting simply out of obligation. Also, don't be afraid to stop the meeting and pray for someone who shares a need or a struggle.

- Most families today are overscheduled and as a result are exhausted and stressed. Question number six this week asks families to take a hard look at their schedules and see if there is something they need to cut out. Be sure to leave adequate time for your group to process this question.

- The "On Mission" component this week asks families to consider who they could serve as a family. This could even be done together by all the families in your group. Serving together creates great memories and bonds the family together.

SESSION 9: what's a woman to do? (part 1)

- Since this is the next to the last week of this study, you might want to spend some time this week talking about what your group is going to do after you complete this study.

- As this series winds down, this is a good time to plan some kind of party or fellowship after you complete the study. Find the "party person" in your group and ask them to take on the responsibility of planning a fun experience for the group. Also, use this party as a time for people to share how God has used this series to grow them and change them.

- For the discussion time this week, Chip is going to ask you to do something a little different. For the first five discussion questions split up into two groups: one for men and one for women. Then, get back together for the final two discussion questions.

SESSION 10: what's a woman to do? (part 2)

- Be sure that everyone is clear what your group is doing next after this study.

- Don't forget to celebrate what God has been teaching you and doing in the lives of group members. You might want to take some time at the beginning of this week's session to have people share how this series has impacted them.

PRAYER AND PRAISE

One of the most important things you can do in your group is to pray with and for each other. Write down each other's concerns here so you can remember to pray for these requests during the week!

Use the Follow Up box to record an answer to a prayer or to write down how you might want to follow up with the person making the request. This could be a phone call, an e-mail, or a card. Your personal concern will mean a lot!

DATE	PERSON	PRAYER REQUEST	FOLLOW UP

DATE	PERSON	PRAYER REQUEST	FOLLOW UP

DATE	PERSON	PRAYER REQUEST	FOLLOW UP

DATE	PERSON	PRAYER REQUEST	FOLLOW UP

GROUP ROSTER

NAME	HOME PHONE	EMAIL

WHAT'S NEXT?

More Group Studies from Chip Ingram

NEW BIO
Quench Your Thirst for Life

5 video sessions

Cinematic story illustrates Biblical truth in this 5-part video study that unlocks the Biblical DNA for spiritual momentum by examining the questions at the heart of true spirituality.

NEW House or Home Marriage
God's Blueprint for a Great Marriage

10 video sessions

The foundational building blocks of marriage are crumbling before our eyes, and Christians aren't exempt. It's time to go back to the blueprint and examine God's plan for marriages that last for a lifetime.

NEW Good to Great in God's Eyes
10 Practices Great Christians Have in Common

10 video sessions

If you long for spiritual breakthrough, take a closer look at ten powerful practices that will rekindle a fresh infusion of faith and take you from good to great...in God's eyes.

Balancing Life's Demands
Biblical Priorities for Busy Lives

10 video sessions

Busy, tired and stressed out? Learn how to put "first things first" and find peace in the midst of pressure and adversity.

Effective Parenting in a Defective World
Raising Kids that Stand Out from the Crowd

9 video sessions

Packed with examples and advice for raising kids, this series presents Biblical principles for parenting that still work today.

Experiencing God's Dream for Your Marriage
Practical Tools for a Thriving Marriage

12 video sessions

Examine God's design for marriage and the real life tools and practices that will transform it for a lifetime.

Five Lies that Ruin Relationships
Building Truth-Based Relationships

10 video sessions

Uncover five powerful lies that wreck relationships and experience the freedom of understanding how to recognize God's truth.

The Genius of Generosity
Lessons from a Secret Pact Between Friends

4 video sessions

The smartest financial move you can make is to invest in God's Kingdom. Learn His design for wise giving and generous living.

God As He Longs for You To See Him
Getting a Right View of God

10 video sessions

A deeper look at seven attributes of God's character that will change the way you think, pray and live.

Holy Ambition
Turning God-Shaped Dreams Into Reality

7 video sessions

Do you long to turn a God-inspired dream into reality? Learn how God uses everyday believers to accomplish extraordinary things.

Invisible War
The Believer's Guide to Satan, Demons & Spiritual Warfare

8 video sessions

Are you "battle ready"? Learn how to clothe yourself with God's "spiritual armor" and be confident of victory over the enemy of your soul.

Living On The Edge
Becoming a Romans 12 Christian

10 video sessions

If God exists...what does he want from us? Discover the profile of a healthy disciple and learn how to experience God's grace.

Watch previews & order at www.LivingontheEdge.org

Love, Sex & Lasting Relationships
God's Prescription to Enhance Your Love Life

10 video sessions

Do you believe in "true love"? Discover a better way to find love, stay in love, and build intimacy that lasts a lifetime.

The Miracle of Life Change
How to Change for Good

10 video sessions

Ready to make a change? Explore God's process of true transformation and learn to spot barriers that hold you back from receiving God's best.

Overcoming Emotions that Destroy
Constructive Tools for Destructive Emotions

10 video sessions

We all struggle with destructive emotions that can ruin relationships. Learn God's plan to overcome angry feelings for good.

Rebuilding Your Broken World
How God Puts Broken Lives Back Together

8 video sessions

Starting over? Learn how God can reshape your response to trials and bring healing to broken relationships and difficult circumstances.

Why I Believe
Answers to Life's Most Difficult Questions

12 video sessions

Examine the Biblical truth behind the pivotal questions at the heart of human existence and the claims of the Christian faith.

Your Divine Design
Discover, Develop and Deploy Your Spiritual Gifts

8 video sessions

How has God uniquely wired you? Discover God's purpose for spiritual gifts and how to identify your own.

Watch previews & order at www.LivingontheEdge.org